SAINTLY DEACONS

Owen F. Cummings

Paulist Press
New York/Mahwah, N.J.

Cover design by Cynthia Dunne
Book design by Lynn Else
Interior artwork by Diann K. Ditewig

The cover design of the Trini Cross with the traditional deacon's stole is courtesy of Deacon Bill Scarmardo for Pax Creations, Inc., www.paxcreations.com, 866-PAX-6373.

Library of Congress Cataloging-in-Publication Data

Cummings, Owen F.
    Saintly deacons / Owen F. Cummings.
        p. cm.–(IlluminationBook)
    Includes bibliographical references.
    ISBN 0-8091-4322-4 (alk. paper)
    1. Christian biography. 2. Deacons–Biography. 3. Church history.
I. Title II. IlluminationBooks.

    BR1700.3.C86 2005
    270'.092'2–dc22

2004022088

Published by Paulist Press
997 Macarthur Boulevard
Mahwah, New Jersey 07430

www.paulistpress.com

Printed and bound in the
United States of America

Contents

Introduction 1

CHAPTER ONE
  Stephen and Philip 5

CHAPTER TWO
  Lawrence of Rome and Ephrem of Nisibis 17

CHAPTER THREE
  Alcuin of York and Francis of Assisi 31

CHAPTER FOUR
  Reginald Pole and Nicholas Ferrar 45

Conclusion 64

Further Reading 67

To Deacon Silvio Mayo
and his wife Mary,
for many years of service
to the Church
in the Diocese of
Salt Lake City

Introduction

What is a deacon? What does (or can) a deacon do? These are fairly common questions, not least for the children and families of permanent deacons. They are good questions, but not easily answered. Growing up in the 1950s in a devout Catholic family, I had never heard of deacons. A deacon was someone on his way to the priesthood, but in the local parish scene he was largely nonexistent. The diaconate was just a step on the way to the priesthood, sometimes literally a "step." On the steps up to the sanctuary in the chapel of Mundelein Seminary near Chicago, where many ordinations have taken place over the decades, are three steps beginning

with "subdeacon," then "deacon," and finally "priest." This was how priestly ordination progressed. Priesthood was the top step.

Then came the Second Vatican Council (1962–65). There was a push at the Council for the restoration of the diaconate as a *permanent* order in the church on the part of some missionary bishops, as well as some prominent European theologians, including the late Karl Rahner, SJ. And so the Council made the decision to restore the diaconate, leaving its implementation up to individual dioceses. In the *Constitution on the Church*, paragraph 29, we read: "The diaconate can in the future be restored as a proper and permanent rank of the hierarchy." In other words, deacons can be *permanent*, not a "step" on the way to the priesthood. The shape of their service to the church was outlined in the same paragraph of the *Constitution* and was to include: the administration of baptism, assisting at and blessing marriages, bringing viaticum (holy communion) to the dying, proclaiming the scriptures—especially the gospel—and officiating at funerals. Deacons, according to the mind of the Council, are to be ministers at the altar, ministers of the word, and ministers of charity.

Most dioceses have restored the permanent diaconate with great results, especially in the United States. Many parishes have a deacon attached to the parish, fully integrated into its life and outreach, performing all the ministries noted above—and more! Many deacons have found full-time employment in the church at both parish and diocesan levels. Deacons are usually known as "Deacon

Cummings" or the "Reverend Mr.," or "Reverend Dr." to distinguish them from priests. Most of them are married, and bring to their service of the church the rich and challenging experience of the vocation of Christian marriage.

There are different ways of thinking theologically about the diaconate in the church, but the way chosen in this book is by looking at *saintly* deacons—men whose example sets the standards of what a deacon's life and ministry should be about. Two deacons have been chosen from different time periods in the church:

- Stephen and Philip, from the first century, the apostolic period (ca. 33–100).
- Lawrence and Ephrem, from the patristic period, the time of the great fathers of the church (100–600).
- Alcuin and Francis from the Middle Ages, a high point of Christian life (600–1500).
- Reginald Pole and Nicholas Ferrar from the sixteenth and early seventeenth centuries, the time when the church in the West was split by the Reformation (traditionally considered as beginning in 1517).

In case you are wondering why we stopped with the sixteenth/seventeenth centuries, the answer has to do with the fact that by this time the diaconate was almost universally understood to be a stepping-stone to the priesthood. Undoubtedly, the Holy Spirit is inspiring saintly deacons in our *own* time, but that will be a project for some future author who will look upon us and our period as the tradition of the church. By examining and probing the life

and contributions of each of these saintly men in our tradition, we shall find answers to what a deacon *is* and what a deacon *does*. Finally, in the Conclusion we shall try to provide a summary approach to these pressing questions about the meaning and purpose of the diaconate.

While not all of these deacons are canonized saints in the Roman Catholic Church, they all displayed "saintly" attributes that *all* deacons should try to emulate.

CHAPTER ONE
Stephen and Philip

*O*ne of the most frustrating experiences for the inquisitive Christian who is trying to grasp the earliest years of the faith in terms of the shape of ministry is to come up against the fact that we have no historically verifiable blueprint of ministry in the first century. We do not possess all the relevant data we would need to provide such a picture. We must be content, rather, with three fundamental observations. First, since the church existed, it must have had some form of ministerial leadership and service. Not only the existence of the church but its rapid expansion into the Greco-Roman world from a Jewish background and matrix demands

Lord Jesus,
Receive...
... Forgive...

a shaped ministry. That ministry may have been more charismatic than finely structured in the first decades of the first century, but there can be no reasonable doubt that there was some definite shape to the Christian ministry.

Second, from such glimpses as we have in the texts of the New Testament, it seems reasonable to guess that the ministry involved the preaching of the good news, the sacrament of baptism, and the celebration of the Eucharist, or to use its earliest name in St. Paul's first letter to the Corinthians, the *Lord's Supper* (1 Cor 11).

Third, from the pastoral letters (1 and 2 Tim, Titus), we can recognize something like the threefold ministry beginning to emerge: bishop, priest, and deacon, but we have no detailed picture.

However, since this book is about saintly deacons, we must try to gather what we can of the diaconate in these earliest years, and in particular the diaconal ministry of Stephen and Philip. The most obvious place to begin our account is with the famous passage from the sixth chapter of St. Luke's Acts of the Apostles. According to Acts 6 (the best thing to do is to read through the entire chapter), the growing community of Christians in Jerusalem had many problems.

The situation seems to have been something like this: The Greek-speaking Christians, the Hellenists, murmured against the Aramaic-speaking Christians, the Hebrews, because the Greek-speaking widows were being

neglected in the daily *diakonia*, what the revised standard version of the Bible translates as "the daily distribution." Responding to this pastoral problem, the twelve apostles insist that they cannot give up the *diakonia*/ministry of the word to serve at table. The decision was taken to choose "seven men of good repute, full of the Spirit and of wisdom" to attend to this duty: Stephen, Philip, Prochorus, Nicanor, Timon, Parmenas, and Nicolaus—all Greek names. The apostles prayed and laid hands on them, a gesture of empowerment and authority. The trouble is that when we read of two of these men acting in the community, Stephen and Philip, they are not serving at table, but are involved in the "service of the word." So before we move on to give an account of Stephen and Philip, let's pause and probe more carefully this important word, *diakonia*, that is, service/ministry.

   To gain further insight, the Acts 6 passage must be set within the wider context of the entire book. The entire narrative of the book, telling the story of the spread of the good news from Jerusalem to the ends of the earth, is described by St. Peter as "this *diakonia*/ministry" (Acts 1:17). Much later on when St. Paul summons the elders of the church of Ephesus to meet him at Miletus, at the end of his missionary journeys, he tells them that he is firmly determined to finish the mission God has given him: "Yet I consider life of no importance to me, if only I may finish my course and the *diakonia*/ministry that I received from the Lord Jesus, to bear witness to the gospel of God's grace" (Acts 20:24). And, when Paul eventually arrives in Jerusalem, he proceeds to tell the community and its lead-

ers "what God had accomplished among the Gentiles through his diakonia/ministry" (Acts 21:19). Both at the beginning and at the end of Acts, the author, St. Luke the Evangelist, wants us to think of the entire work of evangelization, preaching, and building up the church as *diakonia*/ministry.

From chapter 2 through chapter 5 of Acts, the Twelve are represented as constantly in ministry: "And all day long, both at the temple and in their homes, they did not stop teaching and proclaiming the Messiah, Jesus" (Acts 5:42). Then immediately comes Acts 6:1: "At that time, as the number of disciples continued to grow, the Hellenists complained against the Hebrews because their widows were being neglected in the daily *diakonia*/distribution." It is this neglect that leads to the selection and appointment of "seven reputable men" (Acts 6:3). The Twelve were preaching the word and looking after the spiritual needs of the native speakers, the original, Aramaic-speaking community in Jerusalem, "both at the temple and in their homes" (Acts 5:42). These are the *Hebrews* of our text. The *Hellenists* are the Greek speakers, who were not at ease with the Aramaic language of Palestine, the primary language used by the Twelve, and their complaint had to do with the neglect of their Greek-speaking widows, a group whose state in life made them also socially and economically insecure. The Twelve respond to the complaint by saying, "It is not right for us to neglect the word of God to *diakonein*/serve at table" (Acts 6:2).

What does *diakonein*/serving at table mean in this context? The normal understanding has been that it has to

do with food and the necessities of life, "serving at table." There are problems with this. First, in Luke's use of the word, *diakonia*/ministry has to do primarily with the church's *preaching* and *teaching* the good news of Jesus, as we have just seen. It does *not* have to do with waiting at table, serving food like a waiter. Second, the Greek text does not actually say "serving *at* table," but "serving table." So what's the difference? In all probability the Twelve were not talking about serving food *at* table, but rather, *ministering the word* in the Greek language to these Greek-speaking widows gathered at their tables. The Twelve ministered to the larger groups of Aramaic-speaking Jews in the temple and in their homes, Aramaic being probably the original language of the Twelve. But they provided ministers of the word for the Greek-speaking widows, especially when they came together at their tables. "Brothers, select from among you seven reputable men, filled with the Spirit and wisdom, whom we shall appoint to this task" (Acts 6:3). And so the seven were appointed, and when we observe the work they did in the subsequent chapters of Acts, especially Stephen and Philip, they are proclaiming the *diakonia*/ministry of the word. In other words, the church found within itself the ministerial resources to make sure that the spiritual needs of the Greek-speaking widows were met, when they were unable to be met by the mainly Aramaic-speaking Twelve. The Greek-speaking seven were the pastoral solution provided by the mainly Aramaic-speaking Twelve.

It is a commonplace among New Testament scholars today that the men listed in Acts 6:1–6 were not dea-

cons as we understand that term *today*. It was St. Irenaeus (ca. 130–ca. 200), bishop of Lyons, who first referred to them as *deacons* toward the end of the second century. While St. Irenaeus may have been reading the ministerial situation and structure of his own times back into New Testament times, the fact remains that he clearly recognized diaconal service as an important part of the church in his recognition of the seven as deacons. Furthermore, as the word *diakonia*/ministry/service is used various times in the passage, it is natural to associate the seven with diaconal roles. So, let's stay with the tradition and think of them as deacons in some sense of the word. They take on a foundational diaconal role, even though they were not deacons in the formal and specific sense of the word.

The term *deacon* is, of course, used in other texts in the New Testament—Phil 1:1; 1 Tim 3:8–13; Rom 16:1— but nowhere, as we've noted already, are we provided with a clear description of what their functions and roles were in the church. When we come to Stephen and Philip, the best known of the seven "deacons" in the Acts of the Apostles, we find them preaching and baptizing much as the apostles did.

Stephen

The name Stephen is Greek. He was a Jew of the Diaspora, that is to say, from the Jewish communities living outside of Palestine. Stephen is described as a prophet, "a man full of faith and the Holy Spirit" (Acts 6:5) and also

as "full of grace and power" who did "great wonders and signs among the people" (Acts 6:8).

Stephen was accused of blasphemy by some who belonged to the synagogue of the Freedmen to whom he was preaching about the Lord Jesus, and as a result he was brought before the Sanhedrin, the council. False witnesses gave evidence against him, but during the course of his trial we are informed that "all who sat in the council saw that his face was like the face of an angel" (Acts 6:15). Stephen responded to the high priest with a long speech recounting the history of salvation (Acts 7:2-53). The speech ended with the accusatory note that the "stiff-necked people," resisting the Holy Spirit, betrayed and murdered the Righteous One, Jesus (Acts 7:51-52). As a result of this, Stephen was stoned to death.

Just prior to his stoning outside the city of Jerusalem, Stephen, "full of the Holy Spirit, gazed into heaven and saw the glory of God, and Jesus standing at the right hand of God" (Acts 7:55). As he was dying Stephen prayed, "Lord Jesus, receive my spirit" and "Lord, do not hold this sin against them" (Acts 7:60). Finally, we are told that Saul, later to be St. Paul, "was consenting to [Stephen's] death" (Acts 8:1).

There is a certain parallel between the Lord Jesus and his servant Stephen. As Jesus was led before the Sanhedrin for trial, so was Stephen. Both were accused by false witnesses. As Jesus commended his spirit to his Father (Luke 23:46), so Stephen commended his spirit to Jesus (Acts 7:59). Both died just outside the city of Jerusalem. Pious men saw to Stephen's burial (Acts 8:2), in

the same way that other pious men had seen to Jesus' burial (Luke 23:50-55). The deacon Stephen, speaking the word fearlessly, like his Lord, is fully and finally configured to that Lord in his death. As he is dying, Stephen, in imitation of our Lord, prays that his executioners may be forgiven. He is the first to give his life for the Lord Jesus as a martyr—the Christian protomartyr. St. Stephen is the patron saint of deacons. His feast day is December 26.

Philip

Like Stephen, the name Philip is also Greek. Philip had the distinction of being the first to proclaim the gospel in Samaria (Acts 8:5-13). He had much success, both in exorcizing unclean spirits and healing the paralyzed, just as had his Lord Jesus in the Gospel of St. Luke. He carried on the work of the Master. One of his converts in Samaria was Simon the magician, known as "the Great" (Acts 8:11).

In response to an angelic prompting, Philip also converted the eunuch of Candace, the queen of Ethiopia, on a journey from Jerusalem to Gaza (Acts 8:26-40). Philip joined this unnamed Ethiopian treasury secretary running alongside the chariot in which he was reading aloud—the customary manner of reading in antiquity—the prophet Isaiah. Philip, presumably still running because the text does not actually have him get into the chariot, helped the man understand what he was reading in terms of the Lord Jesus, and when they came to a suitable pool of water, they both went down into the water and Philip

baptized him. After the baptism, "the Spirit of the Lord caught up Philip" and he was found preaching the good news in the coastal plain, from the city of Azotus to the city of Caesarea.

In Acts 21:8f we are told that Philip was in residence in this coastal city of Caesarea where he is described simply as "the evangelist." Literally, the term means "one who proclaims the good news," and we have seen Philip doing just that. We are also informed that he had four unmarried daughters who were prophets. Paul, who had witnessed the death of his colleague Stephen, stayed with Philip at Caesarea en route to Jerusalem.

As with Deacon Stephen, there is a certain parallel between Deacon Philip and his Lord Jesus. He preached the word, he healed and cast out demons, as did the Master. He reached out to the marginalized—a eunuch, one who was castrated, and for that reason could not participate as a full member of the liturgical assembly in Judaism. In the most literal sense such a person did not count—but he counted for Philip. Philip was caught up by the Spirit, just as Jesus was throughout his ministry in the Gospel of St. Luke, and caught up as he was by the Spirit, he noticed people in need, especially those who were not ordinarily considered important.

We never hear anything about the five other men upon whom hands were laid. They have vanished into Christian history. However, given the profile of Stephen and Philip, it seems reasonable to infer that the others ministered the Word and baptized in Jesus' name. The very fact that they have vanished from the written pages of

Christian history really says it all. It is the *message* of the good news in Christ that is all-important, not the *messenger*. It is the deacon's willingness to *serve* that is important, not the personal details of his own journey in faith. St. Philip's feast day is June 6.

CHAPTER TWO
Lawrence of Rome and Ephrem of Nisibis

Once we move well into the second century we begin to get a more developed picture of the activity and ministry of deacons in the church. There still is no complete job description as such, but we get enough hints, suggestions, and details to be able to piece the puzzle together.

Apparently, deacons assisted bishops in looking after church property and in the relief of the poor and needy. They brought holy communion to the sick who were unable to be present for the community Eucharist on the Lord's Day. While Christians were being persecuted (that is up to about 312 AD), deacons would also bring the

sacrament to those in prison suffering for their faith. Later in this period (known as the *patristic period*), it became customary for the deacon to proclaim the gospel during the Liturgy of the Word and to assist at baptism. We know the names of quite a few deacons at this time, but two stand out for their reputation as outstanding servants of the church: St. Lawrence of Rome and St. Ephrem of Nisibis.

Lawrence of Rome

Lawrence was one of the seven deacons at Rome during the pontificate of Pope Sixtus II (257–58), the twenty-fifth pope. Lawrence was probably put to death under the Emperor Valerian (253–60) in 258, just four days after the martyrdom of Pope Sixtus II and his four deacons. Valerian had originally been fairly tolerant of the church, but then began a vigorous persecution, ordering Christians to participate in official state pagan ceremonies and forbidding them to assemble in cemeteries, a dearly held custom.

On August 6, 258, the imperial police discovered Pope Sixtus addressing his congregation in the cemetery of Praetextatus, a private burial place not usually watched by the police. Sixtus was probably beheaded there along with his deacons, two of whose names we know, Felicissimus and Agapitus. Some days later, Lawrence was captured and martyred, probably also by beheading, though, according to the received tradition, Lawrence was put to death by being roasted on a gridiron. There is a legend that says that while Lawrence was being roasted alive, he turned to one

of his executioners and joked: "This side is cooked well enough—you can turn me over."

After the Edict of Toleration, Emperor Constantine, about 330, had a church built above Lawrence's tomb in a catacomb. This tomb became a very popular place of pilgrimage. It was a relatively small church, with stairs providing access down to Lawrence's final resting place in the catacomb below.

Emperor Constantine, due to the increasing popularity of the saint, built a large basilica (a church that belongs directly to the pope) on the summit of the hill where Lawrence was buried. Later, Pope Pelagius II (579–90), finding Constantine's original church in a state of total disrepair, tore it down and reconstructed a new basilica at the level of Lawrence's tomb. Finally, Pope Honorius III made these two buildings into one, thus establishing the Basilica of San Lorenzo, much as it is to this day.

Pictures of St. Lawrence were found on gold goblets discovered in the catacombs, and a church was dedicated to him by Pope Damasus *inside* the walls of Rome, the church on his grave-site being *outside* the city, as was the custom with Roman cemeteries. These buildings demonstrate Lawrence's popularity with Roman Christians. In fact, no saint, other than the patron saints Peter and Paul, was more honored by the people of Rome from the time of Constantine on.

Lawrence's memory was preserved, however, not only in church buildings, but also in a number of patristic texts: Cyprian of Carthage, "Letter 80"; Ambrose of

Milan, "On the Duties of the Clergy"; Prudentius, "Peristephanon." Here we will look at Ambrose and Prudentius.

In his "On the Duties of the Clergy" (Book 1, ch. 41.214-15; Book II, ch. 28.140-41), probably composed about 391, St. Ambrose, Bishop of Milan, commends Lawrence as an example to his clergy. According to the testimony of Ambrose, the prefect of Rome asked Lawrence to reveal the whereabouts of the treasures of the church, since deacons to this day are trusted with the church's finances. So, Lawrence brought together the poor and the sick and said, "*These* are the treasures of the Church." The poor, and indeed all the people, *are* the treasures of the church because, in Lawrence's terms, Christ lives in them. Christ lives in them because, according to Matthew 25:31-46, Christ is identified with the hungry, the thirsty, and the poor.

Prudentius, a Spaniard and the greatest of the Latin Christian poets, composed the "Peristephanon," fourteen hymns on selected martyrs. Of these martyrs, six were deacons: Vincent of Saragossa, who died in 304, and often preached for his bishop; Valerian, who suffered from a severe stutter; Augurius and Eulogius of Tarragona; Romanus of Caesarea, martyred at Antioch about 304; and Lawrence of Rome. No doubt when Prudentius visited Rome, he took part in the celebration of the feast of St. Lawrence and visited the basilica dedicated to him. In this poem, Lawrence is presented as the new Augustus, who will be the leader of the spiritual Rome, the heavenly Rome.

The popularity of Lawrence among the Romans and the many legends that gathered about him inspired Prudentius to compose his hymn, which picks up the notion that the Christians had amassed a fortune in silver and gold, stowed away in secret vaults. The prefect was overjoyed at Lawrence's willingness to reveal the church's treasures and gave him three days to prepare.

According to Prudentius:

> [Lawrence] hastens through the city streets,
> And in three days he gathers up
> The poor and the sick, a mighty throng
> Of all in need of kindly alms.
> He sought in every public square
> The needy who were wont to be
> Fed from the stores of Mother Church,
> And he as steward knew them well.

Prudentius knew that the deacon had as one of his roles the dispensing of alms to those Christians in need. The deacon was the steward who knew the poor well and who looked after them. Here was a truly incarnational theology at work. Christ lived in and through these people, these actual people, in all their concrete circumstances. As Prudentius has it, the prefect:

> Would behold them clothed in rags,
> Their nostrils dripping mucus foul,
> Their beards with spittle all defiled,
> Their purblind eyes made blear with rheum.

These ordinary people, in their straitened and anything but desirable circumstances, are Corpus Christi, the body of Christ, *the* treasures of the church. This is Prudentius's way of saying that economics is about people. People, human relationships, caring are the real treasures in life.

It is no wonder that Lawrence became so popular. This deacon knew well that what really counted was people. That is what his martyrdom was about. That is what assured his memorial in the Roman Canon of the Mass. Lawrence in his ministry of charity is a deacon for deacons. His feast day is August 10.

Ephrem of Nisibis (ca. 306–73)

Ephrem was born in or near Nisibis, the easternmost outpost of the Roman Empire just on the Persian border, probably to Christian parents. He was ordained a deacon by Bishop James of Nisibis. When the Roman Empire had to cede his hometown of Nisibis to the Persians in 363, Ephrem went with most of the Christian community to Edessa, in what is today southeast Turkey. In Edessa, which was within the boundaries of the Roman Empire, the exiled Christian community found refuge and a place of safety. There Ephrem established a school of biblical and theological studies. He composed hymns, homilies, and commentaries on Holy Scripture. Many of his writings had an explicitly liturgical setting. We are told by St. Jerome that in some churches Ephrem's compositions were recited after the scriptural lessons in the liturgy. He

was also interested in women's choirs, something of a novelty at the time. As a deacon, he died ministering to victims of the plague in Edessa in 373.

Ephrem wrote theology in the form of poetry, in Syriac, a dialect of Aramaic, very close to the language our Lord himself spoke. Some scholars insist that Ephrem's Syriac verse is so involved and intricate that the only satisfying way of studying him is in the Syriac language! While that is unquestionably desirable, we are nonetheless well served by contemporary translations of Ephrem, especially those of Sebastian Brock of Oxford and Kathleen McVey of Princeton. As a father and doctor, that is, "teacher" of the church, Ephrem is much less well known than others. There are at least two reasons for this. First, the fact that he wrote in Syriac has traditionally made him much less accessible to Western readers unacquainted with the language, but in no way does this mean that Ephrem and his Syriac-writing colleagues are less valuable in Christian theology. Second, the fact that Ephrem was essentially a poet renders him somewhat suspect, even though he was considered the greatest poet of the patristic age. Preference tends to be given to more prosaic systematic theologies in which philosophy is often given the dominant role in the shaping of theology. Western analytic and systematic thinkers have not tended to take with great seriousness those, like Deacon Ephrem, whose theological vision is mediated through poetry.

A major and perduring theme in Ephrem's theological poetry is the inaccessibility of the divine to human

reason. That God exists is knowable, but the nature of God remains impenetrable to human intelligence:

> Thousand thousands stand, and ten thousand
> thousands haste.
> The thousands and ten thousands cannot search
> out the One:
> For all of them stand in silence and serve.
> He has no heir of his throne, save the Son who
> is of him.
> In the midst of silence is the enquiry into him,
> when the watchers [angels] come to
> search him out.
>
> "Hymn on the Nativity," 14

God's throne in heaven is surrounded by count-less ministering angels, standing and serving him. They stand in silence, however, because no one can penetrate the reality of God. God is always more and "other." The only heir the Father has "is of him," that is, reflecting the Nicene doctrine of "one in being with the Father." Only in silence, the reverent silence adoring the mystery of God, may one rightly pursue understanding of God. This is a strong theme in Ephrem:

> If then our knowledge cannot even achieve
> a knowledge of itself, how does it dare
> investigate the birth of him who knows
> all things? How can the servant, who

does not properly know himself, pry into the
nature of his Master?

"Hymns on Faith," 1

What an insight! The servant, that is the human
being, lacks any real and substantial self-knowledge, but
pries into the reality of God. Ephrem views theology not
so much as "faith seeking understanding" because he is all
too aware of the fragility of real understanding, but as
"faith adoring the mystery," reaching out through limited
understanding to adoring in silence the mystery that God
is. Though he does not spell it out explicitly, Ephrem
implies that real knowledge of *self* is the prerequisite for
any knowledge of *God*. If real knowledge of *God* is sought,
it will be found in God's revelation of himself in the person of Jesus:

> If anyone seeks your hidden nature,
> behold it is in heaven in the great womb
> of Divinity. And if anyone seeks
> Your revealed body, behold it rests and looks out
> From the small womb of Mary!

"Hymns on the Nativity," 17

If the hidden and transcendent nature of God is
hidden in Godself, "in the great womb of Divinity," it is
nonetheless revealed and made manifest in the incarnation, "from the small womb of Mary." Here Ephrem bends
the normal lines of thought to speak of the Father having
a womb, and points to the wondrous paradox of the incar-

nation by contrasting that "great womb" with the "small womb" of our Lady. Talking about the womb of the Father is a glorious image and much loved by Ephrem. Here is another passage in which he gives expression to the same theme, but this time encompassing the immanence as well as the transcendence of God:

> The Power that governs all dwelt in a small
>   womb.
> While dwelling there, he was holding the reins of
>   the universe.
> His parent was ready for his will to be fulfilled.
> The heavens and all the creation were filled by
>   him.
> The Sun entered the womb, and in the height
>   and depth his rays were dwelling.
> He dwelt in the vast wombs of all creation.
> They were too small to contain the greatness of
>   the Firstborn.
> How indeed did that small womb of Mary suffice
>   for him?
> It is a wonder if anything sufficed for him.
> Of all the wombs that contained him, one womb
>   sufficed:
> The womb of the Great One who begot him.
>   "Hymns on the Nativity," 13

Here the Son is from the "great womb of the Father," born of the "small womb" of Mary, but he is also found in "the vast wombs of creation." All things came to

be through him and without him was made nothing that was made. Nowhere, no womb of creation, is absent of the presence of the Son, who is the medium of creation, making a Christlike impression on all that is.

It is in the Eucharist that for us Christ comes closest. For the Eucharist, Ephrem also has many beautiful things to say. My favorite passage is this:

> Christ's body has newly been mingled with our bodies,
> His blood too has been poured out into our veins,
> His voice is in our ears,
> His brightness in our eyes.
> In his compassion the whole of him has been mingled
> In with the whole of us.

"Hymns on Virginity," 37

This is a powerful and early representation of the transformation the Eucharist effects in us. Christ is mingled with us through the Eucharist. His transforming presence, poured into us, transforms us from within, so that his voice resounds in our ears, and his brightness in our eyes. One is reminded of the frequently quoted line of St. Teresa of Avila, "Christ has no body now but yours." Ephrem knew that.

Ephrem teaches modern deacons the importance of words and images, especially as they are involved in homilies. The craft of word-weaving is all important and

essential to a deacon. Ephrem exemplifies this to a high degree. He loved words and images and was a true *philologist*, a *lover of words*. One contemporary theologian, Nicholas Lash, has expressed it this way: "Commissioned as ministers of God's redemptive word, we are required in politics and in private, in work and play, in commerce and scholarship, to practice and foster that philosophy, that word-caring, that meticulous and conscientious concern for the quality of conversation and the truthfulness of memory, which is the first casualty of sin. The Church, accordingly, is or should be a school of philology, an academy of word-care." If the whole church is made up of those who love the word and are concerned about theological veracity of words, how much more the deacon, who is given in *Lumen Gentium* 29 (an important document of Vatican II) a specific ministry of the word.

Walter J. Burghardt, SJ, one of the premier homilists in the country, once wrote: "To me, the unprepared homilist is a menace. I do not minimize divine inspiration. I simply suggest it is rarely allotted to the lazy." It is clear that Ephrem was inspired, not in the sense of scripture of course, but through his dedication to communicate as finely and as beautifully as possible the gracious attractiveness of God's word and *Word*. When one begins to think of what must have gone into his preparation of these liturgical poems and homilies that constitute his work, one recognizes in Ephrem a powerful model for deacons in this regard. Ephrem, in his ministry of the word, is a deacon *for* deacons. His feast day is June 9.

CHAPTER THREE
Alcuin of York
and Francis of Assisi

W̱hat might be described as "the golden age" of the diaconate passed away with the patristic period. Even toward the end of that period, however, deacons were still held in high regard, a significant number of them being chosen as bishops and in some cases popes! For example, while Pope Gregory the Great served the church (590–604), a deacon named Constantine was elected as bishop of Milan. Very quickly, however, the norm developed that the diaconate was pretty much the stepping-stone on the way to the priesthood. However, deacons never entirely disappeared. They simply became transitional or temporary, and two

from the Middle Ages are especially worthy of our attention, Alcuin of York and Francis of Assisi.

Alcuin of York (ca. 735–804)

Alcuin is the Latin form of the Saxon name Ealhwine. He was born in Northumbria, England. He was educated in the best traditions of Anglo-Saxon humanism at the cathedral school of York, having been brought there as a child, perhaps due to the premature death of his parents. He tells us that the teachers at the York Minster School, presided over by Archbishop Egbert, were mother and father to him: "It is you who cherished the frail years of my infancy with a mother's affection, endured with pious patience the wanton time of my boyhood, conducted me by the discipline of fatherly correction unto the perfect age of manhood, and strengthened me with the instruction of sacred learning." He became master of the school in 766. Undoubtedly, it was in York that Alcuin developed a taste for one of his favorite foods, porridge with butter and honey. Probably sometime around the same year he was ordained a deacon, and he remained a deacon until he died. He met the great Emperor Charlemagne in 781 at Parma and subsequently became his principal adviser in religious and educational matters.

Charlemagne (ca. 742–814) was the first emperor of the newly established (from 800) Holy Roman Empire. He was recognized as a *new Constantine.* Just as Constantine the Great had furthered the cause of the Christian Church,

lavished benefits on it, and saw himself as its protector, so this new Constantine of the Franks (ancestors of the French) would act in a similar fashion. In addition to his wars and territorial conquests, Charlemagne set about a reform of learning and of the Christian tradition throughout his dominions. This reform became known as the Carolingian Renaissance. The Frankish leader summoned to his court scholars from Italy and Spain, but their leader was to be Alcuin of York. It was to Alcuin that Charlemagne said: "Erect a new Athens in the lands of the Franks." Athens was the very center of ancient learning, and Aachen (Charlemagne's capital city) was to become under Alcuin the new center of learning in northern Europe.

In 782, Alcuin took over the leadership of the palace school at Aachen. The school was for the education of aristocratic young men who were being prepared for administrative civil and ecclesiastical posts throughout the Carolingian Empire. Alcuin's genius lay less in original and creative work than in the careful and systematic dissemination of existing learning. He was a teacher par excellence. He instructed his pupils in the scriptures, ancient literature, logic, grammar, and astronomy. Alcuin not only worked in the palace school at Aachen, but both established and expanded schools in various parts of Charlemagne's massive Frankish empire. The impact of Alcuin's work may be seen in the many texts that survive from this period. As a result of his educational efforts, it would be true to say that Europe would never again face the dangers of barbarism and illiteracy.

One of Alcuin's greatest achievements has to do with the liturgy of the church. Charlemagne wanted to establish uniformity of liturgical practice throughout his realm, and Alcuin was the instrument of his liturgical reform. Liturgical practices had differed from one place to another, but it was Charlemagne's hope that the liturgy would be celebrated in Latin in essentially the same way everywhere. Rome, its liturgical practices and liturgical books, would provide the norm. In this respect Alcuin edited a lectionary (the book of scripture readings for Mass), provided translations of typical patristic sermons for the clergy, most of whom would have been very under-educated by our standards, and revised the Gregorian sacramentary (the book used by the priest at Mass for the Liturgy of the Eucharist) for use throughout the kingdom. He was responsible for introducing some customs from his English homeland into the Frankish liturgy, for example, the singing of the creed during Mass and the celebration of the feast of All Saints, now celebrated on November 1. We get a fine sense of the practical side of the liturgical reforms in the lands of the Franks from the "General Admonition" issued by Charlemagne in 789:

> To priests: That bishops, throughout their jurisdictions, diligently examine the priests, as to their orthodoxy, their [way] of bap-tizing and celebrating Mass; that they may hold to the true faith and follow the Catholic form of baptism; to find out if they understand the Mass prayers well; if

they chant the Psalms devoutly, and
according to the proper division of the
verses; if they themselves understand the
Lord's Prayer, and impart an explanation
of it to all, so that everyone will know
what he is asking of God; that the Glory
be to the Father be sung with all honor by
everyone; that the priest himself, together
with the holy angels, and the people of
God, sing the Holy, Holy, Holy all
together....That [the laity] have their
minds on God when they come to Mass,
and that they do not leave before the
priest's blessing has been imparted.

It is perhaps something of a consolation to realize that
every generation has its difficulties or challenges with what
Vatican II's *Constitution on the Sacred Liturgy* calls "full,
conscious and active participation" in the Mass.

In the celebration of the sacrament of baptism
Alcuin was an advocate of baptism in the threefold formula—
"In the name of the Father and of the Son and of the Holy
Spirit"—and also of a threefold immersion, that is, dipping
the person into the water three times. Despite his master's
customary way of acting, Alcuin was opposed to the practice
of baptizing conquered peoples like the Saxons without ade-
quate preparatory catechesis. Baptism should, of course,
come from free choice and acceptance, Alcuin thought.

Alcuin turned his attention to Holy Scripture,
revised the Latin Vulgate (the Latin version of the Bible by

St. Jerome), and presented the newly revised Bible to Charlemagne on the occasion of his coronation as holy Roman emperor on Christmas Day in 800. We might say that the birth of the Word was being celebrated not only liturgically but also textually.

It is no wonder that Alcuin had an extremely high regard for Charlemagne. He writes:

> As greatly as you rise above other men in the power of your kingship, so greatly do you excel all in honor of wisdom, in order of holy religion. Happy the people who rejoice in such a prince....With the sword of devotion in your right hand you purge and protect the churches of Christ within from the doctrine of traitors; with the sword of your left hand you defend them without from the plundering raids of pagans. In the strength of God you stand thus armed.

Alcuin saw Charlemagne as a duplicate of the great emperor in Constantinople who, like Constantine, was understood to be defender of both church and state, but *more* than a duplicate because he continues:

> There is one power of the Papacy, of the Vicar of Christ. There is another, the lay power of Imperial Constantinople. There is a third, of your own kingship, through

which the Lord Jesus Christ has made you ruler of Christian people, excelling in your strength the two which I have named, more renowned in wisdom, more exalted in the dignity of your realm. See! On you alone all hope for the churches of Christ leans for its support.

This is very strong language indeed from the York scholar-deacon for his royal master, but it affords an exceptionally clear perception of how he saw Charlemagne, sacredly and civilly.

Alcuin retired to the Abbey of St. Martin of Tours in 796, continued his educational projects with some very promising pupils like Rabanus Maurus who was to make his own mark in the Christian tradition, and finally died there on May 19, 804. He was buried in the abbey, and it is worth reproducing in full the epitaph he composed for himself:

Here halt, I pray you, make a little stay,
O pilgrim, to read what I have written,
And know by my fate what your fate shall be.
What you are now, pilgrim, world-renowned,
I was: what I am now, so shall you be.
The world's delight I followed with a heart
Unsatisfied: ashes I am, and dust.

Wherefore think rather of your soul
Than of your flesh; this dies, that abides.

Do you make your fields wide? In this small
    house
Peace holds me now: no greater house for you.
Would you have your body clothed in royal red?
The worm is hungry for that body's meat.
Even as the flowers die in a cruel wind,
Even so, O flesh, shall all your pride perish.

Now in your turn, pilgrim, for this song
That I have made for you, I pray you, say:
"Lord Christ, have mercy on your servant here,"
and may no hand disturb this sepulcher,
Until the trumpet rings from heaven's height,
"O you who lie in dust arise,
The Judge of the unnumbered hosts is here!"

Alcuin was my name: learning I loved.
O you who read this, pray for my soul.

Francis of Assisi (1181–1226)

The former Anglican bishop of Birmingham in
England, Mark Santer, during a homily preached at the diaconal ordination of the present archbishop of Canterbury,
Rowan Williams, spoke as follows: "Of all the saints, the
one whom most people find most Christlike is St. Francis.
And I think it is significant that he was never a priest. He
was ordained deacon, a servant, to the end of his life."

That historically seems to be the absolute truth,
but the only piece of evidence we have of Francis's diaconate comes from Thomas of Celano's account of

Christmas Mass at Greccio in 1223. The exact date of Francis's ordination as a deacon is unknown. But at the Christmas midnight Mass in 1223 Francis chose to be a deacon. The liturgy was celebrated close to the crib, with its manger and straw, its ox and its ass, required by tradition. Francis sang the gospel with his "strong, sweet and clear" voice, according to Thomas of Celano, his biographer. Here is how Michael Robson, OFM Conv., a recent biographer of Francis describes the event: "Greccio became a new Bethlehem. Just as some medieval theologians depicted sin as something that disturbed the created order, so the liturgical celebration at Greccio had cosmic ramifications....The whole night resounded with harmony and the note of rejoicing....The scene was one of religious fervour which momentarily restored the harmony of creation and the outpouring of God's gifts." Our emphasis will be to view Deacon Francis's entire life and ministry as diaconal, and, in particular, his humor (his "holy folly") and his love for God's creation.

Francis's parents were Pietro Bernadone, a wealthy textile merchant, and Pica, of a distinguished French family. His wealth and joie de vivre made him the leader of Assisi's youth. Caught in the intercity feuding between Assisi and nearby Perugia, Francis was imprisoned (1202–03). Serious illness at this time brought about a conversion experience. He heard a voice from the cross of San Damiano, broke off relations with his father, and renounced his considerable familial wealth. It is on this famous occasion that we begin to find Francis in his role of "holy fool." He stripped himself naked, returning all his

possessions to his father, and embarked on what everyone must have thought was a very foolish road indeed. In his remarkable book, *Perfect Fools*, John Saward tells us: "Much that is distinctive in the life of St. Francis corresponds to the spirituality of the fools for Christ's sake. In him we find all the elements of holy folly."

Followers joined him and he received oral approval for his rule by Pope Innocent III about 1210. The Portiuncula chapel near Assisi became the cradle of the new order, and Francis's friend, Clare, was invested there in 1212, and so the Second Order (that is, women followers of Francis) was founded. The preaching of Francis and his friars initiated in Italy a strong penitential movement among the laity, and this developed into the Third Order (laity, men and women, also followers of Francis). So extreme was the poverty aspect of this penitential movement that not only did it appear to be sheer folly to many of Francis's contemporaries, but it created suspicion, trouble, and dissent for the Franciscans for several generations. Another striking view of Francis's holy folly was his missionary zeal, which took him in 1219 during the Fifth Crusade to the Middle East where he tried in vain to convert the Muslim sultan of Egypt, Malik al-Kamil. That seemed extraordinarily foolish to his peers. By all accounts the sultan treated the holy man with courtesy and sent him back to the crusaders' camp—without converting.

Francis's folly found expression in domestic missionary work too. He and one of his companions, Brother Ruffino, on one occasion preached naked and were mocked by the people who thought they had gone mad as

a result of doing too much penance. But, when Francis went on to speak to them of the nakedness and humiliation of Christ, they wept and repented. Folly brought about *metanoia*, that is, *conversion*, or change of heart.

Francis's holy folly in these various manifestations brought about in him what can only be called an "inner freedom," one in which there was no stress or anxiety because he had cast his cares on the Lord and trusted in him with a joyous abandonment. The fundamental and absolute truth about this simple but fascinating man is that he was completely filled, saturated with a sense of God. When you are filled with the truth that is God, you will look strange to other people. As John Saward has it: "In a world gone mad the guardian of truth is invariably dismissed as a raving lunatic."

Francis's love for God's creation finds a fine summary in description in some words of Louis K. Dupre: "Who in thirteenth century Italy had a deeper impact upon his culture than Francis of Assisi, an uneducated man, of average intelligence, but a visionary who saw all creation filled with divine life? After him we looked with different eyes at nature, animals, people. We wrote different poetry and we fashioned different paintings. We lived and loved differently." This is no sentimentalism on Dupre's part, but a judgment that could be amply verified historically. Nature poetry, but in relation to God, comes into its own after Francis. In terms of painting, one thinks of the frescoes of Giotto (1267–1337), which had a huge influence on European painting. Behind these developments, as Dupre says, lies Francis himself, a man in love

with God and with all God's creation. One of Francis's prayers was the short ejaculation, "My God and all things!" To love God is to love God's creation. When one gives oneself to God, *all* creation is drawn into that gift. It is out of this deep conjunction of God and creation that Francis was able to pen the canticle, "Brother Sun," hymning God's praise through all God's creatures, great and small. It is out of this sense of God's deep presence in creation, especially in the incarnation, that Francis could write of Christmas that it was "the feast of feasts; the day on which God clung to human breasts." This is not a quasi-pantheistic reduction of God to his immanence in creation, but a recognition of the consequences of the creation accounts of Genesis, allied to a sense of the cosmic Christ. It is the central Catholic sacramental imagination at work, responding to God's presence everywhere.

Francis's spiritual foolishness for Christ and his consequent sense of inner liberty, his free perspective, his evangelical and missionary zeal provide a paradigm of inspiration for his fellow deacons. His love of God's creation, full of the divine presence and speaking that presence to those who have eyes to see and ears to hear, shows Francis as a sign of the inner connection between church and world.

Francis, while caught up in mystical ecstasy, received the stigmata—the wounds on the hands, feet, and side that Christ was afflicted with on the cross. Not only did Deacon Francis live like a fool for Christ, but he also suffered the same pains as his Lord and Savior. His feast day is October 4.

CHAPTER FOUR
Reginald Pole
and Nicholas Ferrar

The sixteenth century saw the tragedy of the church split in the West between Catholics and Reformers, also known as Protestants. It is a very complex period in the history of Europe as well as in the history of the church. All kinds of factors were at work: economics, the emergence of the nation-state, the easy dissemination of ideas through the invention of the printing press, as well as the widespread desire for reform in the Christian Church. Both Catholics and Protestants now see that, beginning with the Decree on Ecumenism of Vatican II and through

Cardinal Reginald Pole

the writings of Pope John Paul II, people on both sides of the denominational divide were responsible for the schism. Not only that, but ecumenical dialogue since 1965 has helped all Catholics to understand better the intricacies and the subtleties of Reformation theology and has helped all Christians draw closer together, recognizing one another as sisters and brothers. In the Church of England, born as the result of King Henry VIII's separation from Rome, as well as from the Catholic Church, the diaconate continued as it had since the end of the patristic period, that is, normally as a stepping-stone en route to the priesthood. However, even at this time, deacons did not quite disappear altogether. In this chapter we shall consider Deacon Reginald Pole and Deacon Nicholas Ferrar, the former a Catholic and the latter an Anglican. Ferrar remained a deacon, but Pole became a priest. However, he was a priest for just over two years of his long life as a deacon, and may be justly regarded as an example of diaconal service.

Reginald Pole (1500–1558)

Fr. Dermot Fenlon, now a member of the Oratorian community founded by John Henry Newman in Edgbaston, Birmingham, opens his fine book on Reginald Pole with a less than flattering description of the church

on the eve of the sixteenth century Reformation: "At the close of the middle ages the condition of the Church was nowhere considered to be healthy. A papacy preoccupied with politics and taxation, magnificent in everything except religion; an absentee episcopate; an ignorant clergy; an uninstructed laity; a widespread indifference to the spirit of Christianity beneath the forms of established, though sometimes irregular observance: everything had combined to reduce the spiritual life of Christendom to a state not far removed from bankruptcy." Then came the sixteenth-century movements collectively known as the "Reformation," attempts to address these issues, without the clutter of the cumulative tradition, by a return to the Holy Scriptures.

Martin Luther, Huldreich Zwingli, John Calvin, and many others set out a renewal of Christian faith and life, but a renewal that tore apart the unity of Christ's body, the church. In England matters were rather different. King Henry VIII, initially opposed to the continental reforming views, needed a Tudor male heir to his throne, and his wife, Catherine of Aragon, was unable to give him one. Henry sought to divorce Catherine so as to marry Anne Boleyn whose production of a male royal heir he hoped would be more successful. To achieve the resolution of his difficulties in the face of papal disapproval of a divorce from Catherine, Henry declared himself head of the church in England. This is the context for the life of one of the saintliest men in sixteenth century Europe, Reginald Pole.

Cousin to King Henry VIII, Reginald Pole was born at Stourton Castle, Worcestershire, in March 1500, the third son of Sir Richard Pole and Margaret (later

Countess of Salisbury). He received his initial education at the grammar school attached to the Carthusian monastery of Sheen. In 1513 he entered Magdalen College, Oxford, where he was to remain for the next eight years. He was fortunate to be taught by the Greek scholar, William Latimer, one of the men enthusiastic for the new learning that was springing up all over Europe. It would have been during this time that he met Thomas More, canonized by Pope Pius XI in 1935. More and Pole met sometime before 1518, because in that year More thanked Pole for giving him advice on how to deal with sweating sickness. Pole went on in 1521 to a five-year stint of further studies at the University of Padua, Italy. His early education, at Oxford and Padua, had been paid for by Henry VIII and Pole never forgot this. He wrote to Henry: "May God be my witness that never has the love of a mother for her only son been greater than the love I have always had for you."

Returning to his native land after his studies in 1526, Reginald refused, perhaps after some initial uncertainty, to support this king he loved in his divorce proceedings against Queen Catherine. The king, eager and anxious for his support, offered Pole the choice of the episcopal sees of York or Winchester, both wealthy and influential centers, but Pole demurred. A serious rift began to develop between Reginald and King Henry. One result was Reginald's return to Italy in 1532, with the king's permission and pension. He was to remain in exile for over twenty years. His studies hitherto had been largely of a classical nature, but, as he began to mix freely with reform-minded Christian thinkers and bishops, Pole developed

considerable expertise in the study of the scriptures from about 1534 onward. There is strong circumstantial evidence that Pole's biblical studies involved learning Hebrew. He would already have been conversant in Greek from his earlier studies. One scholar writes: "Pole's thought becomes from this date permeated by the Bible." This increased biblical study had to do not only with the historical-critical interpretation of the sacred text *qua* text. Rather, he came to a complete recognition of the sacredness of the text and to interpret his life and times through it. He began, if you will, to "inhabit" the scriptures. In 1535 one of Pole's friends, John Friar, describes him as "undergoing a great change, exchanging man for God."

In 1535, Sir Thomas More and Bishop John Fisher of Rochester were beheaded in London for their opposition to King Henry's divorce and his assumption of the title Supreme Head of the Church in England. More and Fisher were among Pole's best friends. Henry continued to press Pole for support, eliciting from the latter his written private opinion on the divorce, for the king's eyes only, known as *De Unitate*. As he put pen to paper, Pole wept so much that the tears made the ink on the manuscript run. This document was a robust defense of the papacy and the papal position against Henry, and, at the same time, an invitation to the king to repent. In it we find these words: "I can conceive of no greater injury you could inflict upon the Church than to abolish the head of the Church from the face of the earth....Nothing more ignominious could ever have been imagined than this pretentious title of supreme head of the Church in England." The

harsh language was bound to provoke reaction on the king's part, and it did. Pole's brother and mother were executed. When he learned of his mother's execution in 1541 by Henry VIII, he said that God had graced him as the son of "one of the best and most honored Ladies in England...but now he has wished to honor me still more, and increase my liability, because he has made me in addition the son of a martyr."

In 1536 the reforming Pope Paul III made Pole a cardinal, after his ordination as a deacon, and appointed him, with like-minded reformers, to a reforming commission. At this time Pole was part of a small group whose evangelical outlook not only sought institutional reform in the Catholic Church, but ecumenical rapprochement with the Protestant reformers. The upshot of their work was the 1537 reforming document, *Consilium de emendanda ecclesia*. This document stated clearly the abuses in the church and was to offer the program of reform for the Council of Trent.

In 1542 Pole, still a deacon, was appointed one of the three papal legates to preside at the Council of Trent, though the Council itself did not convene until 1545. One of the first things he did at the Council was to remind the episcopal delegates that it was the clergy themselves (that is, deacons, priests, and bishops) who had brought the church to this sorry state of division. He drew up an address that was read to the Council on January 7, 1546, which gave emphasis to two central themes: first, the need for penance and the clergy to accuse themselves, and second, the need to be impartial in the conciliar deliberations.

The evils of the Protestant Reformation and the difficulties of the church flowed from the avarice, greed, and ambition of church leaders. He was not trying to shame the bishops at the Council, but rather to invite them to see the situation for what it was and to repent. Six months later, for reasons of health and perhaps also due to the fact that he did not approve of how some theological issues were being developed—he still entertained some hope of reconciliation with the Protestants—Pole left the Council of Trent.

In 1549 Pope Paul III died. The conclave to elect his successor, one of the longest in the history of papal elections, lasted from November 1549 until February 1550. Though he had no real desire to be pope, Pole received a large number of votes at the conclave and seemed almost certain to be elected. In the ballot of December 5, he came within one vote of being elected pope. However, his openness and sympathy to the Protestant reformers pulled down upon him the suspicion of heresy, sometimes veiled, sometimes all too obvious. Some of the cardinals wished to preempt matters by electing him pope by acclamation, but he would not go along with the proposal. Eventually, Pope Julius III was elected.

About this time, Pole wrote a treatise entitled *Concerning the Supreme Pontiff*. In it he set out his views on the papacy. The pope's principal weapon of excommunication, maintains Pole, was for healing, and not for damnation. For Pole, the papacy grew out of love. It grew out of Peter's thrice-proclaimed love for Christ (John 21:15–19), and Christ's love for his flock, and love should be the characteristic of papal *service* and *leadership*. The pope should

also be a man of poverty and a man of peace, eschewing public honors end enmity between people.

Pole returned to England in 1554 as papal legate. Mary Tudor, known to many as "Bloody Mary," and a cousin of Pole's, was now queen, and she had set about a restoration of Catholicism in her realm. Though he shared the general attitude of most Christians of the day that heretics should be punished and not be allowed to wreak havoc on the body of Christ, Pole's was a policy of moderation and reconciliation. He was not in favor of Mary's policy of repression that involved burning some three hundred heretics at the stake.

Pole was ordained a priest on March 20, 1556, and two days later was consecrated archbishop of Canterbury, the last Catholic archbishop of Canterbury. During his tenure, he began to introduce the reforms of the Council of Trent, which, of course, he knew firsthand as papal legate there. It was Pole, in his Decree to the London Synod, who first introduced the word *seminarium, seminary,* literally seedbed for the training of candidates for the priesthood. Pole's decree was to become the model for the Council of Trent's institution of seminaries in 1563.

Queen Mary died on November 17, 1558, at St. James's Palace in London, and twelve hours later Cardinal Reginald Pole followed her in death in his palace across the River Thames at Lambeth. In response to the suspicions that had shadowed him from time to time, Pole stated firmly in his will that he had always remained loyal and faithful to his Catholic faith and to the See of Rome. As Fr. Dermot Fenlon notes in the epilogue to his book on

Pole: "In many ways his own life was a martyrdom." The example and the ideals of Reginald Pole were those of a humanist and a saint. His service to the church shows him as a model deacon, a deacon *for* deacons.

Nicholas Ferrar (1592–1637)

Ecumenical awareness and commitment are not *options* for a Catholic but *requirements*, especially for someone in Orders. The 1998 *Directory for the Ministry and Life of Permanent Deacons*, paragraph 22, states: "The ministry of deacons, in the service of the community of the faithful, should 'collaborate in building up the unity of Christians without prejudice and without inopportune initiatives.'" It should cultivate those "human qualities which make a person acceptable to others, credible, vigilant about his language and his capacity to dialogue, so as to acquire a truly ecumenical attitude." It is for this reason that we now turn to an Anglican (Church of England) deacon, Nicholas Ferrar, who was ordained deacon so as to be able to lead his own household's prayers and to be given over entirely to the service of his Lord. But he would not be a priest. Ferrar will be little known to most Catholics, but he too is a deacon for deacons.

The best book on Ferrar is that of the Rev. Alan L. Maycock, priest of the Church of England. Ferrar was born in London in 1592, the son of a well-to-do merchant, a friend of Sir Francis Drake and Sir Walter Raleigh, and of a pious and devoted Christian mother. Ferrar's London was the London of Shakespeare: beautiful, but over-

crowded and in places marked by squalor, a breeding ground for the plague. Reputedly, he knew the Psalter (the Book of Psalms) by heart as a young boy, as well as entire chapters of the New Testament, and the scriptures were to remain absolutely central to his spiritual life. He was educated at Clare Hall, the University of Cambridge, where he was regarded as one of the most brilliant students of his generation, the main subject of his study being "physic" or medicine. One biographer points out that Ferrar "needed all his own medical knowledge" as well as his family's care due to the poor state of his health. He was said to be suffering from ague, a malarialike fever marked by shaking, quivering, and sweating fits. For these reasons of health he left Cambridge in 1613 and traveled abroad, visiting Germany, Italy, and Spain. During his travels, he almost certainly came across St. Francis de Sales's book, *Introduction to the Devout Life,* first published in 1608. We can be certain that Nicholas knew it and came to love it, for it was one of the many books bound by the sisters at Little Gidding, his religious community.

After his return to England in 1618, he went into business for awhile, following in the footsteps of his father and brother, and then entered Parliament, but the changes in the political climate in England, along with his own rapidly changing religious aspirations, persuaded him to give up the brilliant career that was opening before him. Apparently, a very fashionable London heiress was being promoted as a suitable wife for Ferrar, but he declined, determined to lead a life of dedicated, chaste celibacy.

In 1625 Ferrar settled at Little Gidding in Huntingdonshire, an estate purchased by his mother the previous year. Members of his family, including his mother Mary and the families of his brother and sister, joined him there and they established a sort of religious community, numbering about thirty in all. He was ordained a deacon by William Laud, then bishop of St. David's, in Westminster Abbey on Trinity Sunday, in 1626. He never wished to become a priest, probably out of a combination of personal humility and a desire simply to serve his community at Little Gidding in daily prayer. On the day of his ordination to the diaconate, he wrote out on a sheet of velum a vow to serve God "in this holy calling, the office of a deacon."

The church at Little Gidding was in poor condition when the community first became established, and it was a priority for them to put it in good repair as the very center of their lives. Over the west door was an inscription that read: "This is none other than the house of God and the gate of heaven." The Little Gidding community lived a life of devout prayer and worked under a strict rule from 1625 until 1646. Matins (morning prayer, also called Lauds) and Evensong (evening prayer, also called Vespers) were said in the church that the family restored at Little Gidding, but the prayer did not end with those canonical hours. At the beginning of every hour, from 6:00 a.m. until 8:00 p.m., there was an office of fifteen minutes in which groups of the community took their turn. The office consisted of a hymn, a number of psalms, and selections from the gospels. The *entire* Psalter was recited every day, the gospels once a month. In addition, two members kept religious vigil every

night from 9:00 p.m. until 1:00 a.m., and during this time again the whole of the Psalter was prayed.

Ferrar's piety and devotion were rooted in the Holy Scriptures and in the *Book of Common Prayer*, the Anglican equivalent to the Roman Catholic *Breviary*. His personal austerity was well known. He himself kept this community vigil two and later three times a week. On the first Sunday of each month, and on the major festivals, the Eucharist was celebrated in the church by the vicar of Great Gidding, with Nicholas acting as deacon. They prepared for this celebration with great care and acts of devotion.

As well as their life of constant prayer, the Little Gidding community was involved in work for the benefit of the whole neighborhood. Three days a week twenty gallons of gruel, a kind of thin porridge, was prepared for distribution to the poor. The members of the community visited both the poor and the sick, ran a dispensary free of charge for the needy, and offered schooling for the children of the local village. They had a miniature almshouse in the community, and offered a permanent home to four poor widows. Little Gidding was the school, the pharmacy, and the basic infirmary for the whole district. Ferrar was intent that everyone in the household should know a trade, and so they devoted themselves to bookbinding. For purposes of recreation, they had a study circle known as the Little Academy in which they told stories and discussed events of the church's year and Christian virtues.

The Great Chamber was the room in which the community assembled for the daily offices (another term for *prayers*). From this room one could look across to the

church outside. On one side was an organ to accompany their hymn-singing, and in the center there stood a table on which rested a Bible and the Book of Common Prayer, containing the liturgies of the church. Around the church and this Great Chamber revolved the life of the community. It was a life of quiet tranquillity and pervasive contemplation. It is vividly described by Alan Maycock:

> The real background, the primary significance and purpose, of life at Little Gidding was the steady, rhythmic routine of prayer and worship and consecrated effort provided in the daily rule of the household. They knew anxiety of the most urgent kind; they suffered distress and bereavement. Serious crises arose from time to time in their affairs; they were never free from worry about money matters; the most varied activities claimed their attention; and, in spite of all, duties were elaborated and works of charity multiplied as the years went past. But we must never forget that, first and foremost, the life of Little Gidding was the life of Mary, who sat quietly at the feet of Jesus, rather than the life of Martha, who was anxious and busy about many things.

Nicholas was the organizer and administrator, spending eighteen out of every twenty-four hours in such a

fashion that his life could be described as one of perpetual prayer. He conducted a large correspondence, planned the details of the community life, and when studying he either kneeled or, like John Henry Newman, stood at a high desk. But it was a well-balanced life, and he constantly recommended to friends that they should lose weight and take frequent exercise, as well as attend to the things of the Spirit. We can truly say that Deacon Ferrar was a minister of the Word, of the altar, and of charity.

In 1633, King Charles I visited Little Gidding and was very favorably impressed with the religious life of the community. A constant visitor to Little Gidding was the poet, scholar, mystic, and man of prayer, Richard Crashaw. He frequently shared the night watches with Nicholas, and found inspiration and nourishment in the joy and regularity of the community's life and worship.

Ferrar exercised a considerable influence on another Anglican theologian who was to renounce public life and become a priest. This was the priest-poet-theologian, George Herbert (1593–1633). They had become friends at Cambridge, each holding the other in high esteem as "his most entire friend and brother." When Herbert realized he was dying, it was to Ferrar that he sent the manuscript of his poems, *The Temple*, with these words:

> I pray deliver this little book to my dear brother Ferrar and tell him he shall find in it a picture of the many spiritual conflicts that have passed between God and my soul, before I could subject mine to

the will of Jesus my Master, in Whose
service I have now found perfect freedom;
desire him to read it and then, if he think
it may turn to the advantage of any
dejected poor soul, let it be made public.
If not, let him burn it; for I and it are less
than the least of God's mercies.

Ferrar was not adverse to burning books and, in
fact, on his deathbed gave orders that crates of books he
had collected during his travels in Europe were to be
burned right away before he died. But this was not to
include the book of his friend, George Herbert. Within
three weeks Ferrar had a few copies printed for private cir-
culation, and soon *The Temple* appeared with a preface by
Ferrar himself, a book that was to exert a more profound
influence upon religious thought and poetry in England
than any other book written during the seventeenth century. Within thirty years of publication *The Temple* sold
20,000 copies.

Nicholas was a staunch Anglican and held some
quite decidedly anti-Catholic views. Thus, he considered
the pope the Antichrist and the Mass an abomination.
Maycock points out that this was standard and stock opinion at this time of polemics, but adds that it is "rather sur-
prising in a man of Nicholas' stamp." On the other hand,
the community and, especially, Nicholas were on very
friendly terms with a local Catholic family living near
Gidding, and they welcomed a number of Catholic priests

from time to time, who spoke of the community in very favorable terms.

The community of Little Gidding raised questions in England of the time. The rising strength of the Puritan movement gave way to the charge of "Protestant nunnery." In one of his last conversations with his brother, John, Ferrar strongly commended the quasi-monasticism that he had established: "It is the right, good old way you are in; keep in it. God will be worshipped in spirit and truth, in soul and in body. He will have both inward love and fear, and outward reverence of body and gesture." Ferrar loved this life and felt that it was important for his church. On Sunday, December 3, 1637, Nicholas received communion for the last time from the vicar of Great Gidding, Luke Groose, as he prepared for death. About three days before his death he told his community that he wanted to be buried close to the west door of the church. On his deathbed on December 4, 1637, he suddenly rose at the time he was accustomed to take part in the religious vigil, that is 1:00 a.m., and exclaimed: "I have been at a feast...at the feast of the Great King." Then he sank back quietly on his bed and died. Alan Maycock describes Nicholas's final resting-place, the place he himself wanted near the church:

> He died in his forty-fifth year, almost exactly three centuries ago. In that retired countryside the church of Little Gidding, with a small burial-ground about its walls, stands in the corner of a field, unapproached even by a pathway; and outside

the church door is the tomb of Nicholas Ferrar, stripped of every mark of identification....It is impossible today to stand by the bare, simple tombstone...without a profound moving of the heart. Here, in this remote and forgotten place, lies buried one of the most saintly men that has ever adorned the Church of England.

The Anglican Nicholas Ferrar, too, is a deacon *for* deacons.

Conclusion

Now we must return to the questions posed in the Introduction to this book: What is a deacon, and what can a deacon do? If you want a really excellent answer, state of the art, as it were, you could not do better than to read carefully through two Vatican documents, both published as one booklet by the United States Catholic Conference: Basic Norms for the Formation of Permanent Deacons and Directory for the Ministry and Life of Permanent Deacons (1998). You will find there laid out in careful terms the threefold ministry of the deacon: (1) Ministry of the Altar, (2) Ministry of the Word, and (3) Ministry of Charity. Each of these

ministries is necessary, each compenetrates the others, and each will find its own manner of expression in the life of a given deacon in accordance with his natural gifts and talents as well as the charism of ordination.

However, the documents are abstract and conceptual, while the lives of the saintly deacons we have looked at are concrete and attractive. These eight men, each in his own way, enfleshes the abstract theology of the diaconate documents. And, when these eight deacons are taken together, they provide us with a very fine picture of what a deacon is and what a deacon does.

- **Stephen,** an eloquent preacher, a witness to his Lord, utterly configured to him so that he dies as the Lord Jesus died, a martyr's death, with final words of forgiveness and trust.
- **Philip,** a powerful evangelizer and healer, father of four prophesying daughters, and a minister of baptism.
- **Lawrence,** lover and custodian of the poor, the *real* treasure of the church, and a martyr.
- **Ephrem,** lover of the Word and lover of words, word-crafter of poetic greatness.
- **Alcuin,** master teacher, lover of the liturgy of the church.
- **Francis,** fun-loving fool for Christ, mystic of God's holy presence in church and creation; receiver of the stigmata.
- **Reginald,** learned scholar, reformer of the church, with a passion for ecumenism.

- **Nicholas,** man of prayer and Holy Scripture, founder of a Christian community.

Together, these men yield a dynamic picture of the deacon as serving the altar/liturgy, as serving the Word, as serving the community in charity.

So, what *is* a deacon? One who *serves*, and through his committed service *invites* and *summons* forth service in the church.

What does a deacon do? Whatever he *can* do, gifted by God through nature and equipped by God through the grace of ordination, and whatever he is *asked* to do by his bishop, discerning and recognizing his natural and grace-filled gifts. The service of the deacon exists and deacons exist to invite service on the part of all who are church. The form and shape of their service are not determined by some period in the past, however much cherished. The Holy Spirit is with the church *now*. As the late Cardinal Basil Hume was fond of saying, "Pentecost is *now* and *always*." The Holy Spirit in the church is right now using deacons in all sorts of ways in our times, to meet the particular needs of our times, and deacons are asked to serve in whatever ways seem necessary to their bishops for building up the holy body of the church.

> Stephen, Philip, Lawrence, Ephrem, Francis, Alcuin, Reginald, and Nicholas, pray for us all, and especially for the deacons of the church. Amen.

Further Reading

Stephen and Philip:

Collins, John N., *Diakonia: Re-interpreting the Ancient Sources*, New York: Oxford University Press, 1990.

Johnson, Luke Timothy, *The Acts of the Apostles*, Collegeville: The Liturgical Press, 1992.

Lawrence of Rome and Ephrem of Nisibis

Brock, Sebastian P., *The Luminous Eye: The Spiritual World Vision of Saint Ephrem the Syrian*, Kalamazoo, MI: Cistercian Publications, 1985.

Burghardt, Walter J., SJ *Preaching: The Art and the Craft*, New York/Mahwah, NJ: Paulist Press, 1987.

Ephrem the Syrian, Hymns, translated and introduced by Kathleen McVey, New York/Mahwah, NJ: Paulist Press, 1989.

Kennedy, Vincent L., *The Saints of the Canon of the Mass*, 2nd ed., Citta del Vaticano: Pontificio Istituto Di Archeologia Cristiana, 1963.

Lash, Nicholas, "Ministry of the Word or Comedy and Philology?" *New Blackfriars* 68 (1987), 472–83.

Alcuin of York and Francis of Assisi

Dupré, Louis K., *The Deeper Life: An Introduction to Christian Mysticism*, New York: Crossroad, 1981.

Ellard, Gerald, SJ, *Master Alcuin, Liturgist*, Chicago: Loyola University Press, 1956.

Francis and Clare: The Complete Works, ed., Regis Armstrong, New York/Mahwah, NJ: Paulist Press, 1988.

Robson, Michael, OFM.Cap, *St. Francis of Assisi: The Legend and the Life*, London: Geoffrey Chapman, 1997.

Santer, Mark, "Diaconate and Discipleship," *Theology* 81 (1978), 179–82.

Saward, John, *Perfect Fools*, Oxford: Oxford University Press, 1980.

Reginald Pole and Nicholas Ferrar

Fenlon, Dermot, *Heresy and Obedience: Cardinal Pole and the Counter Reformation*, Cambridge: Cambridge University Press, 1972.

George Herbert: The Country Parson, The Temple, ed., John N. Wall, New York/Mahwah, NJ: Paulist Press, 1983.

Maycock, Alan L., *Nicholas Ferrar of Little Gidding*, Grand Rapids: Eerdmans, 1980.

Mayer, Thomas F., *Reginald Pole, Prince and Prophet*, Cambridge: Cambridge University Press, 2000.

On Deacons Generally

Cummings, Owen F., *Deacons and the Church*, Mahwah, NJ: Paulist Press, 2004.
Ditewig, William, *101 Questions & Answers on Deacons*, Mahwah, NJ: Paulist Press, 2004.

ILLUMINATIONBOOKS

Other Books in the Series

Little Pieces of Light...Darkness and Personal Growth
    by Joyce Rupp

Joy, The Dancing Spirit of Love Surrounding You
    by Beverly Elaine Eanes

Why Are You Worrying?
    by Joseph W. Ciarrocchi

Appreciating God's Creation Through Scripture
    by Alice L. Laffey

Let Yourself Be Loved
    by Phillip Bennett

A Rainy Afternoon with God
    by Catherine B. Cawley

Time, A Collection of Fragile Moments
    by Joan Monahan

15 Ways to Nourish Your Faith
    by Susan Shannon Davies

Following in the Footsteps of Jesus
    by Gerald D. Coleman, S.S., and David M. Pettingill

God Lives Next Door
    by Lyle K. Weiss

Hear the Just Word & Live It
        by Walter J. Burghardt, S.J.

The Love That Keeps Us Sane
        by Marc Foley, O.C.D.

The Threefold Way of Saint Francis
        by Murray Bodo, O.F.M.

Everyday Virtues
        by John W. Crossin, O.S.F.S.

The Mysteries of Light
        by Roland J. Faley, T.O.R.

Healing Mysteries
        by Adrian Gibbons Koester

Carrying the Cross with Christ
        by Joseph T. Sullivan